Destiny of A Young Woman

Lessons in Purpose

Duchanna Brown

Duchanna Brown

This book contains excerpts from the NIV, KJV, and NLT Bibles.

It also contains quotes and or references to:

"Our Greatest Fear" *Return to Love* by Marianne Williamson, Harper Collins, 1992

Vectors Used:

Created by Art.shcherbyna - Freepik.com

All rights reserved. No part of this book may be reproduced, stored in a retrieval system, or transmitted in any form or by any means – for example, electronic, photocopy, recording – without the prior written permission of Duchanna Brown. The only exception is brief quotations in printed reviews.

Copyright © 2017 Duchanna Brown

All rights reserved.

ISBN: 978-0-9997205-0-9

ISBN-13: 0-9997205-0-3

DEDICATION

To every girl searching for someone to pour into

her the way I used to .

You are gifted.

You matter.

You have something to offer the world.

Let this book be a sign that God has a wonderful

plan for your life.

CONTENTS

PROLOGUE	II
1: PURPOSE	1
2: BE YE SEPARATE	11
3: WHO YOU ARE	24
4: LET IT GO	36
5: NO, YOU'RE NOT CRAZY	44
6: FAITH WORKS	54
7: THE PROCESS	64
8: CONQUERING SELF-DOUBT	75
9: ASK, SEEK, KNOCK	87
10: AN APPOINTED TIME	96
11: GODLY CONNECTIONS	108
12: BE A GOOD STEWARD	120

Destiny of a Young Woman

Duchanna Brown

Prologue

I started writing this book at the beginning of 2016. It took me six months to finish it, and it's taken me even longer to getting around to publishing it. And to think I thought this would be easy, ha.

What I can say after all this time, however, is that God has been faithful. It is my sincerest prayer is that as you read these words that your life will be changed, that you will be inspired to pursue a real relationship with God and that through that connection God will reveal to you all that he has placed within you. I am so excited about what God is going to show to you through this book. I pray that you are edified and encouraged to be all that God has called you to be.

God, Bless You

Special Note: At the end of each chapter I've include some pages for reflection.

Enjoy.

Destiny of a Young Woman

Duchanna Brown

Chapter 1: Purpose

For I know the plans I have for you," declares the Lord, "plans to prosper you and not to harm you, plans to give you hope and a future.

~Jeremiah 29:11 (NIV)~

What is the thing you can't go 24 hours without doing? The activity you immediately think to do in your downtime. Maybe it's more than one thing. My thing is writing. I do it all the time. Sometimes I write about whatever's on my mind, other times I get inspired and write about specific topics that I've been meditating on for a while. It's both a passion and a release for me. It's not only a passion of mine, but I also recognize that it's a gift, as well. It comes to me so easily it's insane. I've always had a way with words when I was a little girl I used to walk around with a notebook and fill it with scribbles that I suppose were words.

It was almost as if I knew even then that writing was what I wanted to do. The older I got, the better I got at articulating how I felt. I didn't recognize it was a gift until people started telling me how good I was at it. It just kind of flowed out of me. What's that passion or talent for you? What's the thing that flows from you without you even thinking about it?

God doesn't just randomly distribute gifts for us to waste them. He gives them to us to demonstrate his glory through us. That thing you do that no one else can do is linked to your purpose. Your gift fills a void in the earth. You fill a space that no one else can fill because God created you to fill it. Purpose is fluid, it's always in motion moving as life progresses , though it may start off as one thing it may develop into other gifts. You might start off thinking your purpose is to make people feel valued, that could branch off into being a shoulder for someone to cry on, and right into counseling. For some of us purpose is no single gift but a plurality of gifts given to us to glorify God. Your purpose is whatever you were put on this Earth to do to bring glory to God, this is God's purpose for your purpose, to showcase his creative mind through you.

If you're pursuing someone else's desires for your life your living beneath your purpose. Living life outside of that which is pleasing to God is a tragedy. Whether you want to be a doctor, a lawyer, a fashion designer or a teacher, whatever your ambition is let it be to the glory of God. An excellent way to ensure that you are pursuing the purposes of God is just to ask God if you are. Pursuing your purpose isn't supposed to be a scavenger hunt. It is through prayer that we find the direction that we need. You can't have destiny without direction, and you won't have direction without prayer.

Your purpose is God's will for your life so if you are looking for your purpose outside of a relationship with Him you'll always reach a dead end. Seeking your purpose without knowing God it's an empty pursuit because you are attempting to enjoy your life's purpose without the One who purposed you. This is why so many people in high positions are unhappy because they got what they wanted, but they missed the person who makes living worthwhile. Being ambitious is fine but be willing to reevaluate that ambition if it leads you outside of a relationship with Christ.

The gifts God has placed inside of you are directly linked to your purpose. Ask Him what your purpose is and don't be upset if it's not what you originally planned for your life. It wouldn't be the first time you've been wrong, and it won't be the last, just trust that what God shows you is better than anything that you could have imagined for yourself. God is Sovereign, and He knows what's best for us.

You were purposed for more. Before you were ever born God had a plan and a purpose for your life, *'Before I formed you in the womb I knew you, before you were born I set you apart; I appointed you as a prophet to the nations.'* (Jeremiah 1:5). Could it be that the reason you feel lost about what you've been put on earth for is that you haven't collided with the catalyst (God) to your destiny yet?

Discovering your purpose is not about a large bank account, a nice car, or a big house though there is nothing wrong with having those things. But discovering your purpose is not about those things, your purpose is meant to point people to God. Take David, for example, shortly after he was anointed king of Israel he fought Goliath and won. This was a part of God's purpose for his life. Listen to the way he spoke about his fight

"David said to the Philistine, *'You come against me with sword and spear and javelin, but I come against you in the name of the Lord Almighty, the God of the armies of Israel, whom you have defied.'"* (1 Samuel 17:45)

David was anointed (purposed) for this fight. In fact, this match was the first of many he'd fight but, his speech pointed to God. He knew that what he was doing wasn't just for him, but it was going to bring glory to God. It doesn't even have to be spiritual, by fully operating in your gift(s) people will look at you and wonder about their gifts. Living out the purpose of God for your life should ignite a passion in those around you to pursue their destiny. Have you ever been around someone with an infectious laugh? Initially, you might not be in the mood to laugh but hearing that laugh causes you to giggle or smile as well. That is the effect purpose has; it ignites your passion, it pushes you beyond where you are. Once you encounter someone operating in their purpose even on a small scale, you will desire to live out God's purpose in your life as well. It's happened to me on more than one occasion, I've encountered people living out their life's purpose, and it left such an impression on me that it influenced the way I spent my own time.

I should mention, since we're just talking, that pursuing your purpose or your destiny is not about a final destination, it's a journey. One of my family's favorite past times is to go on road trips. To me, they were torture, driving for hours is not my idea of fun. My parents, on the other hand, loved being trapped in a car with my siblings and me for HOURS on end because it gave them an opportunity to spend time with us. In retrospect, I get it. The journey was long, but I could never put a price on the memories made during the time we spent together. We got to reconnect in a way that we might not have been able to on a regular day. That's what purpose does for us. It's a journey, as cliché as that may sound, that allows us to reconnect with God's original design for our lives.

If your purpose were just a location on a map then by the time you reached it, you would have nothing else to look forward to, once you arrived your life's work would be complete. Thankfully, pursuing destiny is not a static experience it's continuous, it requires flexibility. There is no limit to what God can do in your life when you surrender your plans to him. So, why can't you? Why can't you live in the abundance of God's will for your life? What's stopping you? The nature of life is change and progression…what are you waiting for to pursue your destiny? Be honest with yourself. If you're not living in all that God has for you, you're not living. Leap and ask God to lead you in His purpose for your life.

God is the creator, provider, protector, friend, artist, etc. We were made in His image; you share the creative DNA of God. (see Genesis 1:27) God can't be boxed into a category and neither can you. Don't limit yourself, pursue all that God inspires you to. He gave you that idea, business plan, that gift for a reason. He gave you that vision, that passion for a purpose don't sleep on it! Don't run from it, pursue it. People are waiting for what you have inside of you. There are people assigned to help you accomplish that dream. People are waiting to hear what you have to say, people whose purpose is waiting to be ignited by yours. Don't go to sleep. Don't ignore those dreams or turn down those opportunities. God has more for you.

God,

I pray that as my sister reads this book she is encouraged. No matter what she's experiencing whether it's one of the more trying times of her life or a season of unlimited opportunity. Let her know that you have a purpose and a plan for her life whether she sees it or not. She need only ask you for revelation of it. Thank you for being an intentional God. Remind her of your promises through these pages and reveal to her who you've created her to be.

In Jesus's Name, I pray.

Amen.

Duchanna Brown

Reflections:

Destiny of a Young Woman

Duchanna Brown

Chapter 2: Be ye separate
Therefore,

*"Come out from among them and **be separate**, says the Lord."*

~2 Corinthians 6:17 (NIV)~

Have you ever heard the saying about the road less traveled? About how narrow it is, and that very few people take it? That's the best description of pursing destiny, isolating. I would be lying if I said it was fun all the time, or if I told you-you would never feel even the slightest bit alone. Desiring more for your life is going to separate you from the pack. It might even drive a wedge between you and your family, but it's still worth the pursuit. Standing out is a characteristic of the believer, and as a young woman in the quest for your purpose, you must embrace your uniqueness and your individuality.

The reason that you don't quite fit in with your friends or with the "crowd" is that you weren't created to. God is the originator of creativity, everything He makes has His unique signature on it. You, young lady, have God's fingerprint on your life. God has uniquely crafted you with a specific purpose in mind that you and only you can efficiently accomplish. However, the only way you can ever truly discover what that purpose is-is by stepping out on faith. You've got to be willing to walk alone, if need be, to accomplish it.

If you were completely honest with yourself, you'd be able to admit that you're different. You've always been. You're not like your friends on the inside even though you dress and play the part on the outside. You know and have always known that they would never truly "get" you. Well, guess what? That's the telltale sign of a person purposed for more and it is my assignment to let you know that it's okay to be different. That it is perfectly fine that you have a perspective all your own. We've all been misunderstood, underestimated, counted out, and rejected at some point or another in our lives.

I spent a good portion of my formative years trying to be like everyone else. I wanted so badly to be accepted. To blend in, to just not be so different. Gradually, I began to understand that it was entirely okay to be myself because God had created me that way for a reason. The world won't end because I have opinions that other people might not always agree with. I recognized that it's okay I can't always relate entirely to the experiences of those around me because my understanding of the world is different than theirs.

Uniqueness is not a curse, it's a blessing. In a world, full of carbon copies being who you are, an original one of a kind masterpiece, is something to be celebrated. You were purposed to be who you are. God, didn't create you, allow you to have the experiences you've had, and your interpretation of those experiences to be like everyone else. He needs you to be you because who you are is an expression of who He is. Genesis 1:27 tells us that we were made in his image and His likeness. If you look at all the diversity in the world, you'll recognize that God is not conventional, He is unorthodox, complex, so immense you could get lost in Him. And He created you, a little piece of Him because the world needs you too.

The nature of our society is to strip you of who you are forcing you to blend into the crowd or fit into a mold of their making. Culture and circumstance often surround us with people who make assumptions about us and our character, limiting us to who and what they think you we. It's vital for you to understand that not only were you made for more, but you are more than who people *say* you are. You are not validated by the opinions of others. You are approved of by God who thought so much of you and desired a relationship with you so, that He sent His only son to die for you. Many people would love for you to shrink to make them comfortable about their own mediocrity.

Don't do it, don't you shrink.

It's not your job to dim your light to suit the darkness in other people. Marianne Williamson pens in the poem "Our Greatest Fear,"

"...*your playing small does not serve the world. There is nothing enlightening about shrinking so that other people won't feel insecure around you...we were born to make manifest the glory of God that is within us.*"

Marianne understands purpose. She recognizes that God had a plan for each of His us before we even knew it. Living anything less than what God intended for you and being anyone other than yourself is robbing you light and dimming your purpose. Surrounding yourself with people who do not recognize or support your purpose is unhealthy. Are those friends who can't even truly see you worth forfeiting the purpose God has placed in you? Is "belonging" worth sitting outside of God's perfect will for your life? I encourage you to read Marianne Williamson's poem after you read this chapter and allow the words to resonate with your spirit. It's powerful.

Here's the unfortunate reality, most people don't know when their season for friendship with certain people is up. And just like if you leave food out of the fridge for a long-time, some relationships (friendship or romantic) can spoil. They not only deteriorate in interaction, but they can also ruin everything they touch. Now, I'm not saying drop all your friends. That's a bit much. I'm saying you need to be conscious about the relationships you allow to go on in your life unchecked. We, as women, are relational beings, meaning we were created for relationship, but we should pay attention to the people we let into our lives. Your purpose is too vital, too valuable to allow people to cause you to forfeit it. You must recognize that no relationship is worth your destiny especially when the person is not someone God called you into relationship with in the first place. Sometimes we get attached to people who really aren't for us. Whatever they're giving you, whatever you believe they are adding to your life is not worth your destiny. Take inventory of the relationships in your life and ask God to show you who is supposed to be in your life and who isn't. There is nothing more destructive to purpose than ungodly relationship.

The most important question to ask next is, **when is it time to walk away from relationship you feel is threatening your purpose?** Well, the first thing to pay attention to are the signs of an unhealthy relationship. The first most obvious sign it's time to separate yourself from a relationship when is it begins to threaten your peace. A clear distinction must be made here because just because your friend says or does something you don't like doesn't mean that they are threatening your peace. Your friend may say something to you in love that you may take offense to, that doesn't steal your peace, it convicts you. There's a difference.

Proverbs 27:17 tells us, *as iron sharpens iron, so one person sharpens another.* Being sharpened involves running a dull object against a sharp object, that friction is uncomfortable. It's painful, but in the end, you're better for it and sharper as a result. When a relationship continually drains your strength spiritually, emotionally, or financially and you are not any better for it, you might need to re-evaluate that relationship.

Another sign you might need to walk away from a relationship is when you begin to feel like you're being torn down by the people you surround yourself with. This can manifest itself as people talking you out of your God-given dreams and plans or reminding you of who you were rather than encouraging who you are and where you're going. If you notice this you'll have to step back and ask God to help you view the whole scope of the relationship. Sometimes we give people a pass on behavior we wouldn't let anyone else get away with because of how long we've known them or how much we've been through together. The truth is it doesn't matter how much you've been through with a person if they are not growing in the same direction as you let them go or forfeit your own growth.

The last reason you may have to separate yourself from a friend or a group of friends is if they are an ungodly influence. This is probably the most crucial reason for walking away from any relationship. **You must guard your purpose at all costs!** It is too precious, too important to leave to the whims of other people.

Especially for people not connected to where God desires to take you. You must make the conscious decision to walk away from all ungodly influences in pursuit of your purpose. By embracing relationships that distract you from the voice and direction of God you jeopardize the fulfillment of the promises of God over your life. You can't afford to make decisions like that over relationships that are not making you a better person. Ask the Holy Spirit to show you what relationships in your life are hindering you from moving forward in your purpose. He will lead you and give you the strength and courage to walk away from relationships that don't have his stamp of approval on it. We'll talk more about relationships that facilitate purpose in a later chapter.

You cannot live in purpose on purpose until you know who you are and have accepted where you've come from, it's only then you understand where you are going. Getting to know *yourself* is scary, trust me. You'll have to take inventory of your strengths and weaknesses and then be mature enough to accept them both good and bad as a part of you. Don't be afraid to have grace for who you are at this present moment. Don't run from yourself by hiding in relationships, careers, even pain. Embrace who you are. Love yourself enough to walk away from relationships (romantic or not) that rob you of your individuality.

Give both your strengths and weaknesses to God, to be used by Him for His glory. Remember, **His strength** is made perfect in *our weakness* (2 Corinthians 12:9).

Perhaps the most beautiful part of this is that God already knows you and already loves you for you. Be unapologetically you.

God purposes in each of us something that is uniquely our own so that when used for his purpose it will bring glory to Him, but having a relationship with Jesus Christ is the only way to get to that. Usually, books like this suggest that you do all this self-improvement work by yourself but as a believer, you have the benefit of knowing the Spirit that made you with purpose. The God who searches hearts, spirits, and motives is willing and able to help you, all you have to do is ask.

One of the many benefits of getting to know God is that as you start to seek Him, in all His majesty, you run into who you were always meant to be. Now, I'm not suggesting that you get to know God for your purpose. God is worth knowing, period. I'm just trying to make sure that you realize that the only way to understand the purpose for which you were created is to get to know your Creator. I dare you to fearlessly and ferociously seek God and see what He shows you in return...you'll be introduced to a version of yourself that you never knew existed.

The Bible tells us to, *seek first the kingdom of heaven and all its righteousness and all these things will be added unto you.* (Matthew 6:33) Jesus was speaking about provision, but it applies to your purpose as well. God is your friend, He will direct you to the people He wants you to be connected to, but you must first seek Him. You are going to have to walk away from some "friends" no matter how good they are to you to become who He's calling you to be. Just because they're good to you doesn't mean they're good for you. Trust God through all of it. Allow Him to lead you and everything else the friendships, relationships, your needs and your wants will be taken care of.

Stepping out on faith, submitting to God's will and living in purpose will require you to stand out from the crowd. The desire to be validated by people must be replaced it with a desire to please God exclusively. You'll have to recognize that this walk might be a little lonely from time to time. You may be misunderstood, overlooked, and mistreated but take heart, you're never alone.

God is not only with you, but He ordained this journey you're about to embark on. He has so much foresight and wisdom that He planned your existence with your specific gifts and talents in mind to execute His perfect Will here on Earth (Jeremiah 29:11). Relationships are important, allow the Holy Spirit to lead you to the ones He's ordained. Don't hold on to people and miss out on all that God has planned for your life. Step out from the crowd. Be separate and stand in your purpose.

Duchanna Brown

Dear Heavenly Father,

Thank you for your daughter who you've placed destiny in. God, I pray that you would give her the strength, courage, and wisdom to walk away from any relationship romantic, platonic, even familial that doesn't look or sound like one you've ordained.

God, remind her that your intentional and if that relationship ends you have something better in mind waiting for her. Give her the boldness to walk away from the crowd and walk toward you so that her purpose will be unlocked. Help her to know that if she's walking with you, she will never walk alone.

In Jesus's Name, I pray.

Amen

Destiny of a Young Woman

Reflections:

Duchanna Brown

Destiny of a Young Woman

Chapter 3: Who You Are

*For **we are God's handiwork**, created in Christ Jesus to do good works, which God prepared in advance for us to do.*

~Ephesians 2:10~

Did you notice that I didn't title this chapter, "who were you?" or "who do you want to be?". That's because the most critical question you need to answer right now is who are you at this present moment. That's the person God will use to execute his perfect plan for your life. Though your past and your future are both very much a part of the bigger picture of your story, all you have to work with right now is the present. In fact, the today is all you ever really have to work with. So, who are you? Do you even know who you are? Have you ever bothered to take stock of who you are and what you bring to the table? Most importantly, are you willing to put in the necessary work to discover and understand who you are?

These are important questions, but I can't answer them for you. Ultimately, you have to decide if finding out these answers are worth it. Deciding to discover who you are is a scary and demanding process, but it should be something you desire to do. Being ignorant of who you are is a disservice to yourself and to others. People without a strong sense of their identity spend a lot of their time pretending to be other people. They spend so much time trying on other people's personalities that they rob the world of knowing who they are.

Discovering who you are will require you to look at what you've allowed to influence your perception of yourself. As you uncover your identity you'll have to sort through the truth about you and throw out the lies you've allowed to control the way you view yourself. Take a step back to figure out who you are in Christ and where you are in life. This is a critical part of discovering your destiny. Your purpose can't even fully be realized until you do this. After you read this chapter, I recommend that you reread it because discovering who you are is one of the most crucial parts of this whole journey. When you know who you are you don't allow your failures and disappointments to dictate your worth or deter you from what you know God has purposed you to do. After you've fought long and hard to realize who you are nothing and no one can cause you to question what you already know to be true. You are purposed and thus destined to become everything God's called you to be.

You can trust that God knows who you were, who you are, and who you will be. He is where finding out who you are begins. All the answers you are looking for reside in your Heavenly Father. Think about your favorite book, if you want to know why and how the characters develop don't you go to the author for understanding? The same goes for discovering who you are. Now, I'm not saying that you'll know everything or that you don't change over time. You are human, you're subject to change. Life happens, and we mature with time, but the core of your identity is found in Christ. He is your sure foundation, the solid rock. You've got to go through him to find yourself. Think back to those three questions I asked you earlier (Who are you? Do you know who you are? What do you believe you have to offer the world?). Did you know the answers immediately? If you didn't, did you even know where to begin when it came to answering them? No? That's because as the creation you have to consult the Creator to understand His handiwork (Ephesians 2:10).

What if I don't like His handiwork? I'm glad you asked. Let's be clear the way you look on the outside has very little to do with the work God is doing in you on the inside. Your looks neither qualify or disqualify you from the purpose God has placed in you. God searches hearts not faces. (Jeremiah 17:10) God is much more concerned about the condition of your heart than He is about the way you look, the way other people think you look or the way you think other people think you look. The truth is what people often reject about us are the very things God has placed within us to add to our uniqueness.

A central point that I must also make is that God took His time when he made you. You are beautifully (fearfully) and wonderfully made. (Psalm 139:14) Before you go running to change everything about yourself learn to appreciate and take care of what you've been given. You might discover that you are pretty dope just the way you are. God took His time with you, learn to love and appreciate that fact about you. Hating things about yourself is equivalent to telling someone who labored in the kitchen for hours to make you a delicious meal that it tasted, "alright." Or worse yet it's like getting up from a full spread on a dinner table, even though you're hungry because you didn't like the way it looked. It's foolish and just plain rude. Your looks and your purpose very rarely have anything to do with each other, but it's your attitude about them both that will influence where God will be able to lead you. If you're more caught up about the appearance of things that don't matter than what God wants to do in your life, you'll miss all that God has for you focusing on what you think you lack. Do us both a favor and choose to believe what God says about you and decide to like what you see in the mirror.

An equally substantial obstacle to understanding who you are is coming to terms with who you were. I know that I mentioned earlier that who you were is of no consequence to who you are, but many people still don't know who they are because they're still trying to fight off the stigma of who they were. The Word of God tells us in 2 Corinthians 5:17, *if any man be in Christ, he (or she) is a new creature: old things are passed away; behold, all things have become new.* (KJV) So many Christians remain bound to the sins of their past. Why is that? I wish the answer were a simple one, but I chalk it up to three factors: environment, Satanic influence telling them that they're not free and people reminding them of the past they want so badly to escape. The chief contributor being that some Christians don't believe that they are genuinely free from the bondage of their past in the first place.

Here's the good news that I'm sharing with you and I hope you'll share with someone else who is struggling with this battle. Your past is in the past! Praise God! What you've been trying to outrun was already overcome on the Cross. I know, it sounds too good to be true but guess what? That's the beauty of salvation; we're freed from sin, our past, and the temptation of future sin. Because of Christ you can choose not to sin. Grace bought us that right and we never have to look back if we don't want to. Okay, back to purpose. I didn't mean to get all preachy, but the Gospel is what makes purpose possible so we might have another praise break soon. When we get there, you have my full permission to put this book down and get your shout in. Okay, back to your past. Stop running from it; you're not bound to it anymore. Yes, it had a hand in shaping you, but it isn't a determining factor in where God is leading you. It's simply a part of the story. Don't run from who you are because of it, embrace it. Take a long look in the mirror, reintroduce yourself and accept the young woman looking back at you. She maybe scarred and a little rough around the edges but she's all you've got, and you owe it to her to love her flaws and all. She's YOU, and if you don't love her, you'll never appreciate anyone else who does.

One more note about your past is that the Devil would love for you to get hung up on your history. In case you weren't aware there is a Devil and he is very real. He is a liar and a dirty cheat, and he wants you to think that he doesn't exist so you can blame everyone else but him for the battles you're fighting. Do not be deceived, homegirl. His calling card is to steal, to kill, and to destroy, one of his best methods of doing so is getting you hung up on your past. If he can get you to spend your present worried about your history, he knows he won't have to deal with you in the future. Don't let him distract you with old news, focus on where you are now. The present is all you have.

Everything we do in our present affects our future. If we eat junk food in the present, we'll be fat in the future, or pleasantly plump as I like to call it. If we feed our flesh now, we will be spiritually weak (or carnal) in the future, and if we spend our time focused on the past now, we'll be doomed to repeat those same mistakes in the future.

The devil doesn't care about who you were; he's concerned with who you will be. If he can get you to forfeit who you will be based on who you were, he's won the battle. Don't let who you were, good or bad keep you from becoming who God intended for you to be. When the enemy, that's who he is, the accuser of the brethren (Revelation 12:10), tries to keep you bound with your past remind him of his future and yours. Do not allow him to torment you with mistakes you've made whether you made them five years ago or five minutes ago. It is not God's will for you to be bound. It is His will for you to walk in the freedom He's already given you. Let go of your past, fight the enemy with the Word, and follow God into your destiny.

The last thing I need you to understand is that you are who God says you are. Look it up in His Word and allow those things to resonate in your Spirit. Before you get to who you will be you must know who you are. This will require coming to terms with who you were. You'll have to forgive yourself and then forgive others for mistakes made and when you're done doing all that you have to be willing to move on. Then, you must overcome your flaws and insecurities. That may take you longer than it took you to read this chapter but it's necessary to position yourself for what's next. Insecurity is a beast that will convince you that you can't move forward because you're not good enough. Let's clear that up right now: YOU ARE GOOD ENOUGH, so, you're going to have to get over that insecurity ASAP. You can't get hung up on your insecurities because it hinders purpose and your purpose is ultimately not about you. The longer you get stuck on the small stuff the longer you keep people from being served by your gifts. Don't forget you have an enemy who is trying his very best to keep you from becoming all that God has created you to be but he's a liar and a cheater and the truth isn't in him. Fight him with the truth of the Word of God. Accept who you are, allow God to use you to for His glory to help you encourage someone struggling with who they are.

Here are some scriptures about who you are in Christ:

A new creature (2 Corinthians 5:17)

Accepted (Ephesians 1:5-6)

Beautifully and Wonderfully Made; God's Marvelous Work (Psalms 139: 14)

More than a conqueror (Romans 8:37)

A Precious Possession (the apple of His eye) (Zechariah 2:8)

Forgiven (Ephesians 1:7)

Loved with an Everlasting Love (Jeremiah 31:3)

Destiny of a Young Woman

Dear God,

I thank you for your daughter. I pray that you would introduce her to who she is in you. God as she seeks you let her find herself. Show her what it's like to be seen through the eyes of her loving Father.

Remind her that she is loved, that she is valuable and that she matters to you. Awaken a sense of worth in her and allow her to see that just like when you created the world you created her, smiled and said she is a good creation.

In Jesus's Name, I pray

Amen.

Duchanna Brown

Reflections:

Destiny of a Young Woman

Duchanna Brown

Chapter 4: Let It Go: The Act of Surrender

Surrender your heart to God, turn to him in prayer and give up your sins—even those you do in secret. Then you won't be ashamed you will be confident and fearless.

~Job 11:13-15 (CEV)~

The next step towards your destiny is a big one, but it's one you are already familiar with. You've already been introduced to small measures of it in the previous chapters. You did it when you separated yourself from the crowd in chapter two and again, in chapter three, when you let God show you who you are in Him. This time around will take more out of you than the other times. This time you'll have to give it all up. This step is one that requires you to relinquish control of your future to God wholly. In this chapter **you're going to have to submit to the will of God for your life.**

Letting go is difficult for most people because many of us find solace in the idea of control. Control creates an imaginary security blanket that allows us to remain comfortable. Most of us believe that once we get ourselves together, our lives will be perfect. As the pilots of our souls, we can manage the amount of pain and disappointment we let into our lives. But let's be honest, if you could control the amount of good or bad that came into your life you would have no need for God, now would you? The more we try to fix our lives, without God, the more of a mess we make of them. Proverbs 14:12 tells us, *there is a way that seems right to a man, but the ends thereof are the ways of death.* We fight to be the captain of our souls only to realize that we are moving towards a dead end. The most sinister part of it all is that you sabotage your purpose in pursuit of what you think is right and you don't even know it. Every time you attempt to control the outcome of your future you interrupt your process, blocking the doorway to your destiny. Submitting to the sovereignty of God is the only way out of this vicious cycle. God is in control. He loves you and would never lead you in the wrong direction. He's on your side even if you don't think He is.

The point of this chapter is not to convince you that surrender is easy. It's to stress that it is necessary. The longer you hold on to the thoughts, behaviors, and actions that exalt themselves over the will of God for your life the longer you prolong the work of God in your life. I know what you're thinking, *Even if I were to let go where would I even begin?* I'm glad you asked. The first thing you need to internalize is that you were never running the show in the first place. The choice to do what's right and how you treat people are about as much as you get control of in this life. If you're wise, you'll allow the Holy Spirit to help you with those decisions as well. The sooner you realize that God has been running the show long before you knew there was a show to run the easier it will be to swallow the reality of your role in God's greater plan. This might mess you up a little bit too but, you didn't even choose Jesus, He wanted you. *You did not choose me, but I chose you and appointed you so that you might go and bear fruit-fruit that will last—and so that whatever you ask in my name the Father will give you.* (John 15:16, NIV) When pursuing your purpose, you must recognize that God is in control. Nothing you attempt to do can succeed without His stamp of approval. We don't even have the right to question how He chooses to run things, but He graciously allows us to ask Him anyways. He is Sovereign, he has the foresight to direct your steps, and he DOES NOT need your help. Our strength is limited; it's God's grace and favor that gets us where we desire to be. Apart from God, we're fruitless.

The next concept you'll have to grasp is that pursuing purpose requires grace. You won't become all that God has created you to be overnight. Be kind to yourself in your failures. There is no such thing as a microwave success, anything that is intended to endure must be developed first. The same thing goes for your purpose. You will fail, make mistakes, be humiliated and have to do it all over again the next day. But if you're learning and you're growing you're moving in the right direction. This process is uncomfortable because you'll have to be entirely dependent on God and be as invested in your growth as you are with anything else. You must allow your faith to stretch, trusting that God's purpose and plan for your life will play out in His time.

Your faith is like a muscle if you know anything about muscles you know that for them to be strong, they must be exercised. This is what happens when you surrender. You're applying your faith. In doing so, your faith will go from mustard seed faith to mustard plant faith, to budding mustard tree faith and before you know it when God tells you something you'll trust Him before you doubt Him but you have to let God be God. If you could do anything to get to where you think you ought to be already, it would have been done, but if you're still waiting, it means that God's still working. Be patient, don't throw a tantrum or run from God because things get hard, run to God because He loves you and He knows what's best for you. Relax, He's got you in the palm of his hand (no it's not just a song from Sunday school, it's biblical) no one can snatch you out of His hand, John 10:28 (read it for yourself, if you don't believe me). This is the time when you must trust God and His word above everything else this includes but is not limited to: your doubts, your fears, your feelings and even the facts. The only thing that matters is the Word God has spoken over your life. He doesn't lie, you can trust Him.

God is the only one who can make what we do prosper as our souls prosper and only what we do for Him in the building up of His kingdom will last. So, *(and I mean this in the most helpful way possible)* please **GET OVER YOURSELF.** Move out of the way and let God use your life for His Glory. Next to salvation, it's the best decision you'll ever make.

Dear God,

thank you for being gracious and kind to us. Thank you for loving us enough to give us memories both good and bad.

Lord, I pray that you will give us the courage and boldness to relinquish control of our lives in exchange for the freedom to trust you.

God, we make the conscious decision to let it go. We decide to follow your lead. Do what you have to do to get the glory out of our lives.

It is in Jesus's Mighty Matchless Name we pray.

Amen.

Duchanna Brown

Reflections:

Destiny of a Young Woman

Duchanna Brown

Chapter 5: No, You're Not Crazy

Trust in the Lord with all your heart and lean not on your own understanding; in all your ways submit to him, and he will make your paths straight.

~Proverbs 3: 5-6~

We've covered some pretty significant things over the last four chapters. Now, we need to address one of the greatest adversaries to your purpose...doubt. Merriam Webster's defines doubt as, to lack confidence in or to distrust. The definition that stuck out to me is fear. Doubt is rooted in fear and if left unchecked your doubt (fears) will lead to unbelief (or the absence of faith). That may not seem terrifying to you, but to me, that's what's really to be feared. Confronting your doubts essential is because if left unaddressed they will keep you from freely pursuing your purpose.

I have to be honest when God started revealing his purpose for my life I thought I was going insane. I was confident that every screw in my brain had come loose. Everything He was showing me lined up with the gifts and talents He had given me, but it just didn't make any Earthly sense. What the world defined as success and God's will for my life did not line up. Not only did His plans seemed impossible for me to reach but I seriously doubted that they would ever come true. Hebrews 11:6 tells us that without faith it is an utter impossibility to please God. Simply put, if you want to live a life that is pleasing to God, have faith in God, there is no way around it. My doubts were not only hindering my purpose, but they were blocking my relationship with God. It's like with any relationship there must be trust for it to work.

Say you're dating a guy and he breaks the trust in the relationship by lying to you. From that point on anything that guy tells you is, in your mind, could be a lie because you were deceived once before. Your trust has been severed, so even if he tells the truth, you're still expecting him to lie. You have no faith in his word which makes it difficult for you to move forward in a healthy relationship with him. Unfortunately, entertaining thoughts of doubt has a similar effect on your relationship with God, and you'll treat him as you would a deceitful boyfriend even though every day of our lives we should be the ones on trial. Isn't incredible that we're the criminals yet we find the audacity to treat God, the holy and righteous Judge as if He's a crook? What a laugh! God is not a trifling boyfriend; He is Alpha and Omega, the author and finisher of your faith. He's the one with the blueprint for your life, and the more you doubt Him, the farther and farther you push away a relationship with Him.

I thought I was crazy when God started laying out His desires for my life. It seemed too big for me to achieve on my own because it was. God, never intended for me to accomplish His plans for my life on my own but the moment he started revealing his purpose for my life I began to exclude him from it. I spent more time thinking, "I can't do this" than "God, I can't do this in my strength but I know that with you all things are possible." This is where we all often make our most significant mistake; we assume that because we can't do it, then it can't be done but God never intended for us to go it alone. His plans for us are centered around Him, but when we exclude Him from his plans, we block His power and highlight that we don't trust him like we say we do. He wants nothing more than the opportunity to show Himself mighty and strong on your behalf, but He has to be given a chance to. He can achieve whatever He has planned for your life with or without your consent but He doesn't force Himself on anyone, we have a choice. He wants to give you the best, but you have to embrace all that He has for you. I wasn't going crazy; I was allowing my insecurities and fears to keep me from adopting the plan God had for my life.

It's clear that doubt hinders purpose, but like all things, God can use it to propel you forward. Doubt can serve another purpose entirely. Doubt can also signify that you're going in the right direction. Fear and doubt are both natural reactions to the unknown. It is also very natural to run away from the things that scare us. However, the truth is that doubt is often a sign that whatever it is that you're afraid of is what God is calling you to.

Everything that you've ever desired/longed for is on the other side of your comfort zone. Doubt often comes to us because we don't know what to expect; it's easier to assume the worst and not to step out on faith than it is to believe God for the impossible the first time. Fear is a sign that you have more confidence in your circumstance than in God. Your worries *are* valid if your faith is in your ability to accomplish what God has called you to do. Dealing with doubt is inevitable, you must go through it to get to what God has for you. It's uncomfortable, but it's all part of the process. I've learned that God often uses our most painful and uncomfortable seasons to produce growth in us. Times of uncertainty can be used by God to cultivate our faith.

Whenever doubt presents itself that is an optimal time to qualify your faith. Do you believe what God has spoken over your life? Or are you going to give in to your fears and allow them to cause you to remain where you are? Doubts, like most negative things, try to present themselves as the truth, but it's just as uncertain as faith is. Your suspicions may be right, but they could also be wrong. Why put faith in what's negative when you could have hope instead?

You must push past your doubt recognizing that your fears have no foundation other than unbelief. I've talked myself out of more than one opportunity just because I was afraid to take the first step. I couldn't see the result and assumed that because I couldn't see the end that I shouldn't even bother starting the journey. That is no way to live your life, and that is certainly not an attitude of faith. Faith believes that things will work out in your favor before you ever physically see them working out in your favor. Just because you can't see it doesn't mean it's not there, it just means you don't see it yet. It hasn't manifested itself yet. Your job is to believe, prepare, and work until it does.

So, here's what you do when doubt begins to plague your mind. First, remind yourself of the promise. *What did God say? Is He still who He says He is?* (Hebrew 13:8) Okay, then you can rest in who is He is. (John 15:4) Don't allow doubt to take root by rehearsing hypothetical scenarios in your head repeatedly because like I mentioned earlier it will become unbelief. Instead, rehearse the truth of God in your mind. After, you've reminded yourself of what God promised you've got to decide to believe God's word over your life. Choosing to believe is important because even though faith is a gift it must be exercised or it'll be weak. You don't have time for weak faith. You are a young woman of destiny; you have things to do.

The work part is essential too because the bible tells us that *"Faith without works is dead"* (James 2:17). If you believe that God is calling you to open a nail salon, you'll go to school to become a nail technician or business school and get the proper credentials. If you believe that God is leading you to become a designer, you'll go to design school and surround yourself with creative people who are already doing what you desire to do.

The point of it all is that doubt is just a scare tactic that Satan uses to intimidate you out of your purpose. He knows that if he can keep you from believing what God has spoken to you, he can prevent you from becoming all that God has called you to be. If he can get you off track from the beginning, he can keep you from bringing glory to God. **DO NOT BE DECEIVED.** God has a plan and a purpose for your life. Doubt qualifies our faith. Don't allow doubt to talk you out of your purpose, shake it off and move in the direction of your destiny. God is able, and you are capable.

Dear God,

Thank you for being gracious and kind to us. Thank you Lord for using all things (good and bad) for our good.

Lord, help us to use our doubt as a tool to qualify our faith. Teach us to combat the lies of the enemy with the truth of your word.

Lord, we ask that you show us your truth through our doubts. Give us the boldness and courage to pursue your will for our lives despite our doubts.

It is in Jesus' Name that we do pray,

Amen

Duchanna Brown

Reflections:

Destiny of a Young Woman

Duchanna Brown

Chapter 6: Faith Works

> **By faith *we understand*** that the universe was formed at God's command, so that what is seen was not made from what was visible.
>
> ~Hebrews 11:3~

I believe it goes without saying that pursuing your purpose requires faith. Hebrews 11:1 defines faith as *"the confidence in what we hope for and assurance about what we do not see."* To be completely honest, for years I heard this scripture and never fully understood what it meant. It was just a bunch of words, they sounded good, but I just didn't get faith. I knew that I was supposed to expect what I believed for, but I didn't know who, or what to believe in. My faith wasn't focused. That may sound crazy, but it was my reality. Faith was a buzzword, but I was afraid that I would never understand faith; could it be grounded in anything more than my emotions? How could I fully pursue my purpose if I couldn't even believe God for it to become a reality? Frustrated and exhausted, I asked God to develop my faith in Him. I prayed, "Lord, give me a fresh revelation about faith!" God began to make plain to me something I believed would evade me forever. So, I would like to share with you what He imparted to me so that your faith may be made whole. If you're like me, you need faith to be more than a buzz word but a guide to what God is calling you to.

Let me begin by giving you *my* definition of faith. **Faith is an awareness of the character of God.** You will never have faith that works until it is focused on God, but you can only believe God when you know Him. My faith became my own when I received this revelation. You will never be able to trust someone you don't know. You wouldn't trust a stranger with your credit card, would you? In the same way, you can't put total trust in God when you don't know Him. How can you trust a God you neither know nor have a relationship with? The answer to that is you can't. You must first build a stable relationship with Him because relationship is the foundation for trust.

Could it be that you don't trust the call of God on your life because you don't know the God who has called you? You don't know His character, his intentions, His heart towards you, and His passion for you. You don't know Him so you CAN'T trust Him with your destiny. If God's presence in your life isn't evident, it's impossible to believe in Him to move in any way. You may believe in yourself, you may believe in things, but you don't believe in Him. You will never be able to realize the destiny placed within you if you don't know the God who is calling you. It's a real tragedy that we often want the call of God without a right relationship with Him. But you will never get the things of God, the way He intends, without God.

The question is, *how do we get to know God so we can put our faith in Him and not in ourselves or our circumstances?* Well, the answer is multi-layered. First, you've got to establish a consistent prayer life. You don't have to do anything dramatic or out there, but you must pray, preferably, without ceasing (1 Thessalonians 5:16-18). You must be plugged in always. The ability to tap into the presence of God is such a privilege, one most Western Christians take for granted because we've always had access. There was, however, a time when humanity needed a Savior which is what makes what Jesus did so incredible. We don't require a priest or a sacrifice to dwell in the presence of God. There was a time when sin cut us off from God. We were not able to commune with God the way we are able to now and so we must treat it as the privilege it is. Through communication with God, we can get explicit instruction from him. Keep the line of communication open. You have too much riding on this relationship to shut God out. Abide in His presence, and He'll lead you to your future.

Getting to know God also requires a knowledge of His Word. His Word is who He is. Everything you'll ever need to know about God and His thoughts towards you is in His word. It is in His word that you'll learn that he is faithful to the faithful (Psa. 18:25) and that He never forsakes the righteous (Psa. 37:25) and all the other beautiful attributes of His character. God is outlined in His Word, and it is your responsibility to take the time to get to know Him for yourself. As you seek God, He will make Himself known to you. *You will seek me and find me when you seek me with all your heart.* (Jeremiah 29:13) (NIV)

Once you've come to the knowledge of who God is you will be able to put your faith to work. James 2:17 says, In the same way, faith by itself, if not accompanied by action, is dead. The next verse says, to paraphrase, some people will argue that some have faith, and others have good deeds, but James says that people will know what you believe not by what you say but by what you do. As you believe God to manifest your destiny your faith will motivate you to keep going. It is your faith that will pilot every endeavor, every venture, everything connected to your future.

Your purpose is married to your faith; you're going to have to believe in God to see His promises for your life come to pass. Hebrews 11: 3-31 tells of all the things that we can do by faith. *By faith*, we understand (v. 3), *by faith* we can sacrifice and be commended by God like Abel, *by faith* we speak through our example even long after we are gone (v. 4), and *by faith*, we obey like Noah and Abraham did (v. 7, 8). Every name mentioned in Hebrews 11 (The Faith Hall of Fame) is a testimony of what is possible if we trust God with our lives. We can fulfill the purpose placed before us only by, and through, faith in God. Your destiny belongs to God, so your faith must be grounded in nothing and no one other than Him. He desires to promote you and use you in both secular and religious arenas, but you must consider Him who made the promise faithful (Heb. 11:11).

The last thing I'll say before we move on is that faith is not lazy. Your actions are a direct reflection of what you believe. Faith is more than just wishful thinking, it's operating [acting] in belief. It's more than just saying *God, I trust you. God, I believe you. God, God, God...* it's understanding that God has equipped you to do whatever He's purposed you to do. It's your responsibility to take the first step and be committed to working until the process, and your purpose meets His promise. If you believe that God has called you to write a book, start brainstorming and outlining it. If you believe God has called you to start a fashion line, get a sketchbook and start designing one. Or take sewing classes to learn how to make clothing and begin finding fabric that you like. **Faith doesn't wait to be greenlit to believe God's promises, it provokes us to do before we see.**

Hebrews 11:13 says it like this:

*All these people were still living **by faith** when they died. They did not receive the things promised; **they only saw them and welcomed them from a distance**, admitting that they were foreigners and strangers on earth.*

Faith makes room for what it sees from a distance. God desires our total belief in Him. Trust in Him is more than just saying we believe, but it is also coming into agreement with what God has spoken to us with actions that are in alignment with His Word. That means that we cannot be contrary in our behavior. We can't say we trust God and doubt Him. We can't say that we believe

God and live in fear or remain stagnant. We must bring every part of our being into alignment with the will of God for our lives.

Trusting God requires more from us than just lip service, it requires sacrifice. You can't say your believing God for things you're not willing to make room for. Faith will require you to look crazy for a while, but in the end, it will be worth it because God will get the glory out of your decision to trust Him. And isn't that the point of realizing your purpose in the first place? So, that you can give back to God what He's so graciously given to you? The revelation of purpose leads to action. You have got to put your feet to the ground. Yes, preparation is necessary for whatever God is calling you to, but the work you put behind your purpose will demonstrate if you genuinely believe what God has spoken over your life. Your activity or lack thereof is a good gauge of where your faith is.

Heavenly Father,

*We thank you that you are a God worthy of our trust. **You. Are. Faithful.** And so now we come to you full of faith that what you've spoken over our lives will in deed come to pass. Not because we're so great or perfect, but because you are faithful to your word. You honor it above your Name. God, we make the declaration along with the conscious decision to live lives in which our actions and words line up with our faith in you.*

God, we pray that as we get to know you we will have a more profound faith in you. That you will expand our faith and increase our expectations of you. Thank you for being a God we can trust. We love you and we're ready to put our faith to work.

It is in Jesus's Mighty Name we do pray,
Amen

Reflections:

Destiny of a Young Woman

Duchanna Brown

Chapter 7: The Process

He will sit as a refiner and purifier of silver; **he will purify** *the Levites* **and refine** *them like gold and silver. Then the LORD will have men who will bring offerings in righteousness, and the offerings of Judah and Jerusalem will be acceptable to the LORD, as in days gone by, as in former years.*

~Malachi 3:3-4~

In most congregations across America, the promise is preached without the process. Sleepless nights and dreary days, the moments in which you feel like you're the only one who has ever gone through anything ever, are left out of many Sunday sermons. I want to shine a light on the gloomier parts of this journey, not to discourage you but to encourage you to live through them. Those moments of despair matter too. It happens to all of us whether we acknowledge it or not.

A process is promised. God will never promise you anything without process attached to it. The process is what God uses to refine us, clean us up and transform us into the women He created us to be. I'd define it as <u>what you didn't expect you'd have to go through to get what God promised you</u>. The Bible is full of examples of them. From Moses to David to Daniel there are countless stories of how God uses the process to prepare men and women for their purpose.

One of my favorite stories is Ruth's. Ruth's story started off pretty good, she was happily married to Mahlon, living with her in-laws and though the Bible doesn't explicitly say it, we can infer, she was relatively happy. Everything was going well until her husband, her brother-in-law and her father-in-law all got sick and died. This series of unfortunate events left Ruth, Naomi (her mother-in-law), and her sister-in-law as childless widows. The childlessness in this story though not often highlighted is significant because children represent legacy and now, none of them had one. Orpah, Ruth's sister-in-law decides to return home to live with her parents. Ruth, however, loved Naomi so much that she begs her to let her return to Bethlehem with her, Naomi's hometown. It is there that we follow Ruth's process, and their kinsman redeemer Boaz restores Ruth and Naomi. God gives Ruth a new husband and Naomi a grandson named Obed. It is through Obed's family line that we get Jesus.

Ruth and Naomi *had* to go through the process before they could reap the benefits of the promise. Had they not dealt with their tragedy they would have never been able to appreciate the blessing that Boaz and later Obed were to them. Ruth's process helped her to fulfill her purpose which was to be the great-great-great (there are a lot more greats in there) grandmother of Jesus! Had she given up and went home after she lost her husband she would have missed out on the fantastic blessing God had in store for her. You can't skip the process. It's through the process that you are prepared for your purpose.

Why do we have to go through the process anyway? Well, I'm glad you asked. Have you ever taken a test and not studied for it? I have, and I've been immature enough to pray and ask God to give me knowledge for a test I didn't prepare for and wasn't interested in learning material for. The process is a gift because it blesses us with the time we need to develop. God is Sovereign, all-powerful, Mighty, Wise, the list goes on and on, and He could slip you the answers if He wanted to but He won't. What would you learn if you never experienced anything?

Psalm 119:71-72 says, *It was good for me to be afflicted so that I might learn your decrees. The law from your mouth is more precious to me than thousands of pieces of silver and gold.* The psalmist understood that his experience pushed him to learn God's Word. It's through God's word that we learn about God, His goodness, His provision, and His protection. That's what the process will do to you; it will push you closer to God. It will force you to face yourself and discover your potential. You'll come to realize that God desires to pull purpose out of you and He will do it by any means necessary. It's through pressure and affliction, through hard times and frustration, that God gets our attention. The process not only prepares us but it forces us to depend on God in ways we probably wouldn't have otherwise. The process is laborious because it kills your flesh and your dependence on yourself. The process is hard because total surrender is hard.

The process of writing and editing this book has been difficult. It seemed like with every chapter came some new disappointment or frustration. Every time I felt discouraged or depressed or lonely, I would turn to God to help me through what I was dealing with. I would ask the Holy Spirit for guidance. There were times when I felt like I was on a tightrope and one wrong move could spell the end for me. Fortunately, I realized that I wasn't going to hit the ground because God is the net. God has us in the palm of His hand. Nothing can pluck us out, not a broken heart, loneliness, failure, and certainly not this process. (John 10:28) The process is designed by God to cultivate you and develop you even if it feels like it's hurting you.

The process is not painful the entire time, and it won't be smooth sailing the whole time either. The experience is designed to include both the good and the bad to make you better. You've got to go through it. You've got to experience it all. The incredible highs and the terrible lows because it's through this process that you learn to appreciate the fullness of God's goodness. I've cried more tears than I could catch but God understood every one, not one escaped His sight. He's a good Father; He knows His kids from the inside out. He knows what's bothering us before we even figure out what's wrong with us. He can be trusted with our cares and our fears, all of them, even the ones we can't tell the people closest to us about. You learn that in the process.

I used to believe that God wasn't present during my seasons of trial, that God was present for the good stuff and somehow missing for the bad. I didn't always see how he could use bad situations for my good. His word says He's a very present help in our time of need (Psalm 46:1). He's concerned about you and me. (1 Peter 5:7) He's with us through it all, and He promised to be with us always even to the end of time (Matthew 28:20). However, it's not His will that we sidestep the process.

Outside of process, you have to accept that trouble is promised to humanity. (Job 14) Suffering is a part of life, but God is not ignorant of our pain, He not only cares but He understands. The process doesn't produce pride; it's meant to humble you, to remind you of your humanity and to magnify why we need God. Don't lose sight of who God is in all of it. Remember, that He disciplines those He loves (Hebrews 12:6) and He loves you. He loves you so much He led you to this to bring out the best parts of you and kill all the things that have been holding you back for so long. Trust Him through the process; you'll be better for it.

The last thing I want you to learn is that you must embrace the process to get through it. I think that's the part of Ruth's story that inspires me the most. Ruth had every reason to complain. Her mother-in-law was miserable, she was a young widow, and she had every reason to give up right where she was, no one would have blamed her. In all of that she never once complained. She was patient in her affliction, and she appreciated what she did have. She didn't run from her problems, but in humility, she faced them with a faith that not even Naomi could muster. We should all aspire to have that same attitude when faced with our process.

DO NOT, I repeat, DO NOT avoid the hard stuff. Don't try to take shortcuts past the valleys, around the hills and away from the battles. I'm not going to lie to you; it's going to be painful. It's going to be painful because who you are is changing into who you will be and that's going to require some stretching and growing in ways you never imagined. If you've ever worked out before you know that before you get the ripped arms and the six-pack abs, it takes lots of eating right, exercise, and some weeks of soreness before you see any results for all your hard work at all. But you don't stop working out because it's painful because you know the result is the body you've always wanted. This is how you ought to view your process. Pain demands to be felt so no matter how you try to avoid it's going to be felt in one way or another. Don't try to numb it, don't distract yourself from it, endure it because the process, *produces perseverance; perseverance, character; and character, hope. And hope does not put us to shame, because God's love has been poured out into our hearts through the Holy Spirit, who has been given to us.* (Romans 5:3-5)

With every experience whether good or bad you are learning, growing, being prepared for a purpose only you can accomplish. God, created you for this time and He doesn't make any mistakes. Don't be discouraged, be of good courage, and wait on God, while you wait He will strengthen your heart and mind. (Psalm 27:14). I'll close this chapter with the words of my friend the Apostle Paul. *I know what it is to be in need, and I know what it is to have plenty. I have learned the secret of being content in any and every situation, whether well fed or hungry, whether living in plenty or in want. I can do all this through him who gives me strength.* (Philippians 4:12-4:13, NIV)

Endure.

Duchanna Brown

Hey God,

It's us again. We just wanted to say thank you for loving us enough to put us through a process that will make us better. Help us to see the beauty in this struggle. Remind us when we're frustrated and want to quit that you've put in us the strength and determination to keep going.

Help us to see that if we're ever running low we can get the strength we need from you. Remind us that your wisdom is available to us we need only ask and you'll give it to us freely.

God, I thank you for being with us throughout this experience, when we get tired or weary help us to remember we're not in this alone.

God, we thank you in advance for your finished work in our lives. You're making diamonds out of us in this process so we can shine for you. Thank you!

We love you and we honor you.
It is in Jesus' name we do pray.
Amen.

Destiny of a Young Woman

Reflections:

Duchanna Brown

Destiny of a Young Woman

Chapter 8: Conquering Self-Doubt

*Therefore, my beloved brethren, **be ye steadfast, unmovable,** always abounding in the work of the Lord, for ye know that your labor is not in vain in the Lord.*
~1 Corinthians 15:58~

Admittedly, when God gave me the title to this chapter, I struggled with sitting to write it. How can someone who still struggles with self-doubt provide advice to someone else who may be struggling with the same thing? Well, God is kind and gracious. I asked Him what He wanted me to write and He gave me some good stuff so let's dig in, shall we? I've already dealt with doubting God back in Chapter 5. Now, it's time to deal with doubting yourself. Let's first define self-doubt. Self-doubt is a lack of confidence in one's self and one's abilities according to Google. Not to be confused with low self-esteem which we'll also discuss later in this chapter because it's almost impossible to talk about one without the other.

Now, the negligent thing to tell people dealing with self-doubt is to "believe" in themselves. It's a pretty basic answer to something that's a bit more complex than we often acknowledge. As someone who has struggled with both self-doubt and low self-esteem I can tell you that believing in yourself is a lot easier said than done. There must be more to it than that. I wish I could say that I have this part of my life mastered, that every day I wake up I feel like I can do anything but I don't. Honestly, I don't think anyone has this part of life mastered. We like it when people believe that we do, but we don't. Even the most confident people must face those voices in their head that are judging them a lot harsher than anyone is. It's our shared struggle, a part of the human experience.

Many things contribute to self-doubt, but nothing adds to it more than failure. Thomas Edison, had it right when he said, " I have not failed 10,000 times. I have simply found 10,000 ways that didn't work." He didn't allow his failures (what happened to him) to distort his view of himself (what he was capable of) because he realized that his failures didn't define who he was. He could separate his worth from what he was attempting to accomplish. He believed enough in what he was doing to keep trying because he knew every failure brought him that much closer to success. Sometimes we put too much stock in what has gone wrong in our lives and not enough in what has gone right. There are several sides to a story, you just need to pick one that encourages you to continue in the direction of your purpose. Tell yourself a new story, a story where you win.

Tackling self-doubt is not straightforward. It takes practice to combat the negative thoughts that threaten to rob your self-esteem, but you have a right to fight for what's yours. Self-doubt is founded in two things God doesn't dabble in, the flesh and fear. Doubting what God has placed in you is not God's will for your life. The decision is yours to believe what God says about you and rehearse that instead of all the lies Satan has told you. Practice getting up in the morning and looking in the mirror as you get ready for work or school or whatever and speaking well of yourself. Declare who God says you are and declare over your life the person you believe He's calling you to be. (i.e. "I am smart", "I am healthy", "I am wealthy", "I am the apple of God's eye", etc.) Say it out loud even when you don't feel like it. The Bible tells us that life and death reside in what we say. (Proverbs 18:21) What you say about yourself, your purpose, and your family has power. Which do you want, life or death?

Healthy self-esteem doesn't develop overnight. It requires a concentrated effort. You must decide to love yourself for who you are every day. You are good enough. God didn't make a mistake when he created you; He planned your existence long before you were ever born. Be confident in that. Don't doubt what God has placed inside of you. He has deposited purpose in you, and He has every intention of getting it out of you. You are capable of being precisely who He made you to be. Your gifts, ideas, efforts are no less valuable than the next person. He intends to bring the best out of you, but your perception of yourself has got to change. If anyone should be rooting for you or in your corner, it should be you. Be your cheerleader, mascot, and the stadium full of fans...you get it. You don't need anyone to validate the call, whatever that call is, on your life, if you're waiting for people to approve what God has told you-you'll be waiting for the rest of your life.

If God took the time to speak to you about what He had planned for your life, He isn't waiting for your friends and your family to approve. Follow the voice of God. Don't allow negative people or your negative perception to deter and distract you from what God has told you to do. It's easy to think, "If God told me to do it then it's going to be easy." Wrong, *because* God took the time to reveal your purpose you're going to have more opposition than ever. You think the Devil wants you to pursue your mission? People are going to come out of the bushes, fall out of trees, go out of their way and overstep their bounds to discourage you from what God has called you to do. **Pursue it anyway.**

Satan will use anyone and anything to deter you from your purpose. A few months before I started writing this book my mom and I ran into a family "friend" at a local grocery store. We weren't particularly close to her, but we had always thought of her as a nice woman. So, when I told her that God had called me to Seminary, she proceeded to tell me that medical school was where I should be going because if I went the Seminary route, I would be broke. I was shocked. Then talk about this book came up and she proceeded to discourage me and tell me that people didn't "know" me, so naturally, I shouldn't write it. I was infuriated by the time we finished talking to her, but in her mind, she thought she meant well. However, that conversation only fueled what I already knew to be true, I never asked her for her approval. I knew what God told me and I wasn't going to allow someone who I didn't even know to keep me from doing what God had only told me to do. People are not who you need to be looking to for validation, Jesus is. He will lead you, guide you and direct you.

In Matthew 6:2-4, Jesus reminds us that we shouldn't do things for people's applause and adulation because their approval is the only reward we'll have to look forward to. However, if we do the things of God in secret and God will reward us publicly. People are fickle, they're all around you when you're up but nowhere to be found when you're down. Don't abandon God, who is always for you, for people who can't decide whether they are for you or against you. God placed that dream or desire in you. Don't forfeit it for finite people with no insight into what God has planned for you.

Be steadfast and unmovable in your resolve to pursue God's purpose for your life. Do not waiver. No, you aren't those people you admire who are successful and wealthy doing what you desire to do. Guess what; *they* aren't *you*. The only difference between you and them is that they believed enough in themselves to tirelessly pursue the purpose God had placed on the inside of them. You don't have to be Oprah. Be you! That's more than enough to accomplish all that God has put in you. I don't want to be "the next" anybody. I want to be me. I want to create my lane, and you should want to blaze your own trail too. Not for fame, fortune and all that other stuff. Those things are great, and I believe God wants us to have those things, but your worth is not wrapped up in what you have. Your worth is completely independent of the amount of money in your bank account, the clothes you wear, the way you look or the people you know. Your worth is found in Jesus Christ.

Finally, let's address the demon of low self-esteem. Let's get one thing clear, low self-esteem is the Devil's way of reminding you that who you are in Christ is a threat to him. He understands that if you began to believe in yourself and the power of Christ in your life you'll pursue purpose and homeboy is not trying to see that happen. Your self-esteem should be based on more than your physical appearance. We get hung up on that part because we live in a world that equates what we look like to success or failure. Beauty equals good, virtuous, happy. Being unattractive is equated with a low quality of life somehow. Unfortunately, most people get stuck on how things look and never move past it. God, on the other hand, looks at the heart. (1 Samuel 16:7) Here's the truth: **your worth is not subject on people's opinions of the way you look, behave, think, or speak.**

Think about it this way, opinions are based on experience and experience-dependent on exposure, if a person's environment and experience haven't exposed them to how dope you are you can't hold that against them. More importantly, you shouldn't hold it against yourself. Just because a person or people can't see how great you are doesn't make you any less exceptional. Maybe they're not supposed to see it, and that's okay too. You cannot, however, put your purpose on hold because of it. Beauty is not in the eye of the beholder it's in the eye of the beheld. Don't allow a person to dictate to you your value.

Finally, don't doubt yourself based on anything outside of yourself. Life happens to us whether we are choosing to live it or not but what we allow to affect our view of ourselves is wholly our decision. Your worth isn't based on what happened to you it's based on what Jesus did on Calvary. Somebody willingly died for you! He loved you so much He took off deity and put on humanity just to save you from yourself! Do not allow people who wouldn't even hold the door open for you dictate to you how you should feel about yourself. Recognize your worth.

The Holy Spirit is within you. (John 14:26) You are capable. You are talented. You are equipped to do whatever God has placed you here to do. You are beautiful, just the way you are. There's no one in the world like you. There will never be another person in the world who will be able to be your brand of beautiful.

God made you and was pleased with what He made, get hip and start loving yourself. Change your mindset (the way you see yourself) and watch your life change.

Duchanna Brown

Heavenly Father,

We come before you humbly asking that you'd forgive us for doubting what you've placed within us because of what other people have spoken over our lives.

God, we ask that you renew our minds. Wash us clean with your word and show us who you've called us to be. Show us what we are capable of with your power backing us.

Give us a new perspective on our failures and help us to be teachable vessels for your glory. We give you our insecurities and we ask that you replace them with security in you. We love you and we honor you.

In Jesus's name, we Pray

Amen.

Destiny of a Young Woman

Reflections:

Duchanna Brown

Destiny of a Young Woman

Chapter 9: Ask, Seek, Knock

*Ask and it shall be given to you; **seek** and you will find; **knock** and the door will be opened to you. For everyone who asks receives; the one who seeks finds; and the one who knocks the door will be opened.*

~Matthew 7:7-8~

To discover and live your purpose, you must earnestly and sincerely seek the face of God. God is the one who makes life worth living and purposes worth pursuing. He is our source, and He is our strength. He leads, guides, and directs us to become all that He's called us to be. God uses people to fulfill His divine purpose in the Earth. He desires to use you as well, but you've got to accept His will for your life. Proverbs 3:5-6 encourages us to trust in the Lord with all our hearts and lean not on our understanding. If we acknowledge Him in all our ways, He will direct our paths. You can't find your purpose without direction, and you can't receive direction until you've submitted your will to God.

Ask. Ask God to show you what He has planned for your life. The Bible tells us He won't withhold good things from people who walk uprightly (Psa. 84:11). He has the power to give to us, and it's our power to ask for it. The Word of God tells us that we have not because we ask not, so why aren't you asking? Are you afraid that He'll answer or do you feel like you're undeserving of what you're asking for? If He gave you the desire for it, then He wants you to be daring enough to ask. Ask with the expectation that what you've asked Him for you will receive. Go to God with confidence; it is your privilege and right as a believer to approach the throne of grace boldly. What if I told you He's waiting for you to ask?

Think of it this way; He's a father who delights in seeing us be all that He's created us to be. He wants us to have every blessing He has stored up for us. God has storehouses full of the things He desires to give us but we are sometimes too scared to ask, and we miss out on His heart for us. I get it, being blessed is phenomenal, but sometimes it can be scary. It's a massive weight to carry especially because God loves to show off. Blessings from God the Father expose you, not to embarrass you but to bring Him glory. He revels in our success because it is a direct reflection of His love for us. It's incredible that we serve a God so generous and so loving. One who wants nothing more than to bless us beyond our wildest dreams. We, however, must be willing to ask. God's power is only limited by what we're ready to believe Him for. What's the worst that could happen if you ask God to lead you in your purpose? Are you afraid that you might find it? Are you worried that you might have to be uncomfortable to get it? Sis, He has so much more for you. If you ask Him to reveal to you what that is you might be shocked by what you find out. Ask Him to reveal His will for your life, and you might find the very thing that you've been looking for.

Seek. Seek His unchanging face. So often we seek the council of books, conferences, and our favorite daytime talk show hosts. These avenues of counsel are helpful, but they are not the Source of the insight they provide. Nothing they share with the world is all their own. It came from somewhere. It came from God, whether we're aware of it or not. Why would I go to the store for information about a product when I could go to the product's manufacturer? That's who God is, the manufacturer of the dreams, visions, desires and the purpose He's placed in your heart. Though godly counsel, sound sermons, even this book have their place the first and final reference to check this information with is God through His word and prayer.

The Word of God tells us to *seek first* the kingdom of heaven and all its righteousness, and everything that we need will be added unto us. (Matthew 6:33) The first part of the equation is seeking God. Now, let me warn you this seeking thing is no joke. It's going to require some determination, not because God desires to hide from you but because it doesn't benefit Satan to let you seek the face of God. The enemy will use anything and everything to keep you from what God desires to give you. Expect opposition from every direction from friends, from co-workers, and especially from your flesh! When you do face opposition, be encouraged to continue to seek Him.

Matthew 5 tells us, blessed are those who hunger and thirst after righteousness for they shall be filled. God is a rewarder of those who diligently seek Him (Hebrews 11:6), and He desires to be known as much as you do. If you're in a place where you've lost the desire to seek Him pray that He will reignite the passion you once had for the things of God. If you've never been a place of that kind of passion, pray that He would ignite a fire in you to honestly know Him for real. The Holy Spirit will lead you as soon as you let Him. I know what you're thinking, what does this have to do with my purpose? It has everything to do with it. You must be in right relationship with the Purpose Giver to fulfill your purpose. Seek Him, not the job. Seek Him, not the paycheck. Seek Him, not the beautiful house, the expensive car, or the amazing wardrobe. Seek the Lord, and He'll make your purpose more than just a career choice, He'll make your life worth living.

Knock. I can't tell you how many opportunities I've missed because I refused or was afraid to knock on a door. When God leads you to a door to knock on there is something behind it for you. Don't allow fear to cause you to avoid it; you NEVER know what or who God will use to help you accomplish His purpose in your life. He knows exactly what He's doing, exactly how everything is going to play out. Trust that every door He leads you to will open if you're bold enough to knock.

No, you're not qualified for the job but knock anyway. The word of God says that those whom He justified He also qualified, so there's no need to look for credentials He's already given you. No, you don't look the part but knock anyway. Jesus didn't look like the Messiah to the Jews that didn't negate the fact that He was and is the Savior of the world. No, you don't know all the right people, but if God is for you, it's more than the world that is against you. No, you don't feel like doing it, you don't feel good enough, you don't feel capable. The list of reasons why you shouldn't knock could go on forever. Knock anyway, and the door will be opened. God is not ignorant of your realities, but when it's your time to walk into all that God is calling you to nothing will be able to stop you. Knock anyway and watch God show you that He's not limited by our finite perceptions, society's opinions, or even our insecurities. He will help you fulfill your purpose, but you have to do your part in asking, seeking Him and knocking.

Destiny of a Young Woman

Heavenly Father,

Thank you for giving us a right to ask you for what we desire, to seek your face, and to knock on the doors you've placed before us. Help us not to covet what other people have whether it be their purpose, things, or relationships when we haven't even asked you for our own things.

God, give us the boldness to ask knowing that if we ask you'll answer. We thank you in advance for your purpose for our lives being realized for your Glory. Help us to remember that our pursuits are for your glory. We're so grateful that when we ask we'll receive, when we seek we'll find, and when we dare to knock you'll open doors in our lives that we never dreamed we'd walk through.

We love you and we Honor you

***It is in Jesus's Name I do pray,
Amen.***

Duchanna Brown

Reflections:

Destiny of a Young Woman

Duchanna Brown

Chapter 10: An Appointed Time: God's Timing

*Write down the revelation and make it plain on tablets so that a herald may run with it. For the revelation awaits **an appointed time**; it speaks of the end and will not prove false. **Though it linger, wait for it; it will certainly come and will not delay.***

~Habakkuk 2:2-3~

We've covered a lot of ground so far. I feel like every chapter is more important than the last and I guess, in a way, they are. Like I mentioned in an earlier chapter as I write and you read we're both learning. I want to fulfill my purpose just as much as you do. I'm glad we could take this journey together. This chapter is for those of you who may be like me, impatient. Sometimes it's hard to trust God when you have anxious tendencies. It's even worse when you have a habit of viewing things from a very cut and dry, black and white perspective like myself. God makes big promises but rarely does He tell us how much we'll have to go through to receive what He's promised us. So, with this chapter, He just wanted me to remind you to trust His timing.

I pray for patience often because I can wait for some things, but there are other things that I want when I want them. I can sometimes be like the people from a famous commercial I often see on television screaming out of windows, "It's my purpose, and I need it now!" If I were to be completely honest with myself, however, if God gave me the career, the husband, the family, and the ministry right now, I probably wouldn't have the discipline to take care of it all. In fact, I'd probably crack under the pressure of it all and walk away. I wouldn't be a good steward of it because I haven't gone through the proper training required to maintain and grow the things I desire.

King Solomon's bride in Song of Songs advises the daughters of Jerusalem not to awaken love before it's time on more than one occasion (2:7; 3:5; 8:4), her advice reigns true not just in matters of the heart but in every area of our lives. Seeking things out of season is like picking an apple before it's ripe. You won't enjoy it nearly as much as God intends for you to because you picked the fruit too early. There are things that God desires to do in you before you ever see the fulfillment of the promises He's ordained for you. In fact, those things are all a part of the fulfillment of the promise. He's preparing you. Your job is to stay focused on the goal and keep a right attitude through the process.

I used to wonder why God would send messages to me either through people, through dreams or through speaking to me directly, weeks, months, or sometimes years in advance before those promises were ever even close to being fulfilled. Why would He have me believing Him for something three years before its time? It's simple really, hope. Romans 8:24-25 says, *for in this hope we were saved. But hope that is seen is no hope at all. Who hopes for what they already have? But if we hope for what we do not yet have, we wait for it patiently.*

I would have never hoped for the things God has promised me if I hadn't had a revelation of the promise before I saw it. I would have never had the faith to believe if I didn't have to wait patiently for it. You see, my dear friend, there is indeed a method to the madness. The process we discussed in Chapter 7 must take place, or you won't have the character to be a good steward of what God places in your care. God is a good father, and every good father wants what's best for his child. A good father also knows what their child can handle and when they can handle it. God is a God of order. 1 Corinthians 14:33 in the King James Version reminds us that God is not the author of confusion, but of peace. The NIV says He's not a God of disorder. He's got it all laid out, but you have to trust His timing. He knows better than you when you'll be ready for what He's promised you. He chooses when to tell you about what He has for you because He wants you to prepare.

Think about it this way; God placed the desire within you to pick up this book about purpose. Any time before now would have been too soon because you weren't ready to be receptive to what He had to say to you. Any time after now would have been too late. He's positioning you for where He plans on taking you, but you have to be prepared for it first. You even have to be prepared to endure the process. It's during the time of preparation that you get the opportunity to cultivate your gifts and nurture your craft. It's during the preparation stage that God often develops in you the character needed to accomplish His purpose in your life effectively.

Your season of preparation builds the patience you need to wait on Him and the strength you need to trust Him. While you wait become your own project. Ask God to show you your strengths as well as your weaknesses if you don't already know them. Hone in on your strengths while you develop in your areas of weakness. By identifying these things, you will be prepared for the next step so that when the time comes for elevation, you'll already be confident about what you bring to the table. No one can tell you who you are and they certainly can't tell you who you're not when you've taken the time to get to know you.

A sign of whether a person trusts God or not is their attitude towards their situation. I used to think faith was decreeing and declaring things and though that's a part of it, it's not the whole experience. Faith is not a feeling; it's a decision. It's the decision every day to choose to trust God with **everything**. That means even the things you don't want to trust Him with. It's the conscious decision to give every worry, every care, every concern to God, daily. It's combating fear with faith through prayer, praying without ceasing and reminding yourself that God is still in control. It's renewing your mind daily and allowing God to break down the misconceptions you've had for years about Him, yourself, and others. This type of trust in God causes you to have peace amid your greatest trials and joy when you have every reason to cry. It's with this trust you can see beyond what's in front of you to a Savior who desires nothing but the best for you.

Your attitude during this waiting period is critical because it will either make what you're going through miserable or a breeze. Okay, so say you're at a restaurant waiting for a table, just a table, not food. You and everyone with you is starving, and someone with you is complaining the entire time. "What's taking so long?!", "I'm hungry!", "When are we going to be seated?". They're stopping waiters as they walk by to ask them how long the wait time is. They're trying to speak to the manager so they can be seated faster. Here's the kicker, you've only been waiting for 10 minutes!

Scenario number two, same situation, same circumstances except this time your annoying friend isn't there it's you and your favorite people waiting and talking, laughing and catching up. The conversation is *good*, so good that when the buzzer goes off for your table one of the other parties waiting has to tell you that your buzzer is going off. Which experience was more enjoyable? The one where the person complaining made everyone miserable? Or the one where you weren't as focused on the wait as you were on the people you were waiting with? I think we could both agree that the second experience is the more enjoyable one, not to mention it probably made the wait time seem a lot shorter. This is the will of God for your life that you don't get so bogged down by the weight of the wait that you overlook who you're waiting with and who you're waiting for.

God wants you to get to know His heart for you in this in-between time. He wants you to recognize that everything He's taking you through is only to bring you closer to Him. It's all a setup. He just wants your heart. Don't get so focused on the wait that you miss out on all you could be doing with Him while you're waiting on Him. The journey to purpose and the waiting period are not separate entities; they are one in the same. God gives us the promise which is beautiful and meant to be enjoyed, but the road trip to what He's promised is intended to be appreciated too. There's a misconception about success in both the world and in the church. To most people success is achieving, you're one BIG goal but victory, to me at least, is taking small strides in the right direction. It's those positive as well as negative experiences that make up your overall success.

The Bible says it this way,

And we know that in all things God works for the good of those who love him, who have been called according to his purpose. (Romans 8:28)

He's working while you're waiting, so let Him work.

My friend, I know it's cliché but trust in the timing of your life. Trust that you serve a punctual God who knows exactly where you are and exactly where He's taking you. He's not making this up as He goes along. He's been doing this God thing long before you started doing you. He has a blueprint laid out for your life, and He desires to see that you live it out. Use the time He's given you to learn, nurture your talents, mature, and prepare for what's next. What is for you (career, relationships, family, etc.) won't miss you. It has an appointed time.

You have a set date with destiny. God has orchestrated it so well that you don't have to call an office to book it or e-mail a secretary to schedule it. It's already been planned, not only will you not miss it but you can't miss it. He's birthing in you something that the world desperately needs, something so important that only you can do it. So, don't rush it. Take your time. Your table isn't ready yet. Be patient with God and with yourself. He's not only doing a work in your life, but He's also doing a work in you. You didn't think this was solely about a paycheck, did you? When the time is right, and everything works out the way God promised you it would you'll be grateful that you were patient with yourself and with Him. I encourage you to ask God to help you not to run ahead of Him but to be patient enough to wait for His best.

Destiny of a Young Woman

God,

help us to wait on you, with You. We know now that it's easier to trust you when we focus on you, so help us to be mindful of where you are. Give us the focus necessary to not get distracted by things that really don't matter. We'll wait on you because you're worth the wait.

Thank you for loving us so much that you're willing to take us through what you need to make us into the powerful world-changing young women you've called us to be. We love you, we love who we are and we love who we are becoming.

In Jesus's Name I pray,

Amen.

Duchanna Brown

Reflections:

Destiny of a Young Woman

Duchanna Brown

Chapter 11: Godly Connections

A friend loves at all times, and a brother is born for a time of adversity.

~Proverbs 17:17~

 Life has a way of coming full circle. Earlier, we talked about walking away from ungodly relationships and crowds. Now, we'll discuss the type of company you should be keeping. The people you surround yourself with is just as relevant to your purpose as your process, God's timing and who you are in Christ because the people you keep company with says a lot about where you're headed in life. I have a friend who always says, "show me who your friends are, and I'll show you who you are." Your friends, like your family, influence you a lot. They can expose you to amazing things, or they can introduce you to things that cause you more harm than good. Your friends are your extended support system. You can often share with friends stuff about your life that you don't feel entirely comfortable sharing with your family. Not only are they your support system but they're your council. Their opinions matter to you. I don't know too many people who are friends with people whose opinions they don't respect. Might I add, you are probably not friends with anyone whose opinion you don't respect enough to consider?

In this life, you can only hope for a few real lifelong friends. They may not all bring the same qualities and ideas to the table but they are for you, and you're for them. The Word of God tells us in Proverbs 17:17 that *a friend loves at all times*. That means they love you when you have nothing to offer them and they love you when you're able to give them the world. Their friendship is not dependent on what wealth you have, it's grounded in who you are. Whether you're right or wrong, they stand with you and always tell you the truth in love because they want what's best for you. They see you for who you are and love you regardless of what people have to say about you. A true friend defends you at all times because what happens to you affects them too. The point is purpose is tied to people. So, my question for you is who are you connected to?

I've never really had to seek out friends. Even when I was a moody teenager, it seemed like the more I tried to get rid of my friends the more "friends" I made. So, I've never had a problem making friends the problem

I've had is keeping them. Now, if you are a purpose-driven person, you'll understand this. It's not because I've always been a terrible friend even though those middle school years were rough. It's because when my so-called friends wanted me to stand with them in the crowd, I couldn't help but stand out, and can I be honest with you? Everyone can't handle being friends with a person like that, but if you're a person in pursuit of your purpose, that's just who you are.

I wrote Chapter 2 about being okay with being alone because this journey will get lonely sometimes, you may even have to leave your best friend behind for a season, but it's so that you can receive all that God has for you. Here's a quick side note: By now I hope that if you aren't already saved, you've considered getting to know Jesus. Now, that guy is a terrific friend. I wanted to make it a point to say that there is no lack in God. Everything in Him including friendships and relationships are good. I have to point this out because anything that's unhealthy and isn't bettering the people involved in it is not of God. Do not be deceived. If every time you get around a person or group of people and you feel like your energy is being sapped or you feel like the life is being sucked out of you, you should recognize that those relationships are not of God. If every time you talk to them, the only thing they have to impart into you is "tea" (or gossip), that's not your friend; they're a counterfeit version of what God wants for your life. Believe me, if they are always talking to you about somebody they're probably talking to somebody about you. Pay attention, sis.

If every time you end a conversation you feel worse than when you first started talking to them, girlfriend... THAT. IS. NOT. YOUR. FRIEND. The Bible tells us that, as iron sharpens iron, so one person sharpens another (Proverbs 27:17). If you feel dull every time, you're around certain people you might want to reevaluate who you're spending your time with because who you spend your time with determines the trajectory of your life. If their friendship is not making you better, it might be making you worse, and it will stunt your growth. If it's not healthy, thriving, flourishing, it's not a godly connection, and it would behoove you to get while the getting is good. God don't bless no mess.

I had to share that because as women, especially as young women discovering who we are not only in Christ but in general, we tend to sacrifice who we are or what God is calling us to for people. We don't want to be considered the "bad friend" for walking away from foolishness. But, I would rather be the "bad friend" with peace of mind than the "good friend" with other people's filth clogging up my spirit and blocking God's glory from being revealed in my life. I'm speaking from a place of experience. When I was a sophomore in college, I started hanging out with a "new" crowd. They were fun.

As individuals, they weren't bad people, but when we got together, we would influence one another to be people I don't think any of us actually wanted to be. No one really wanted to lead, everyone (including me) was content with following. It was the "I'll go if you go" mentality which historically has never gotten anybody anywhere but in trouble. I allowed my desire to "fit in" to blind me from a very real, very scary reality that I was unequally yoked. If I continued hanging out with them not only would I miss out on the greatness locked inside of me, I would die and go to hell over people. Talk about a reality check.

My junior year of college we would meet up in the room we met up in every night to waste each other's time it was a continuation of a sophomore year tradition (we spent ungodly amounts of time together, I'm talking 7+ hours a night). I specifically remember being in that dorm room and praying, *"God, there has got to be more to life than this. You have to have more for me. I grew up learning about you, and I know you didn't intend for this to be my life. If you don't get me out of this I'll die here, maybe not physically but definitely spiritually."* And I'm so grateful that in that moment God heard me and not even a month later I had a huge falling out with two people in the group and I haven't looked back since. I thank God that He gave me enough sense at that moment to recognize the people I surrounded myself with didn't match the places He planned on taking me. I know you love your ratchet friends, but you have to love God and yourself more. At least, enough to see what else God has in store for you.

Okay, so we know what ungodly connections look like but what do godly connections look like? Well, first let me define what a healthy friendship is. A healthy friendship or relationship is one in which both people benefit from the relationship. A healthy relationship is never unbalanced, it is mutually beneficial. After being in unhealthy friendships for years, a healthy friendship was different for me. It was weird to be friends with a person who cared enough to tell me the truth in love regardless of how hard it was. My new friends loved me not only in word but in action as well. One of my best friends I've only known for a little over three years, but my life has been significantly enriched by our friendship. I know that she can be trusted with whatever I share with her and vice versa. I can genuinely say that I'm better with every conversation whether it's serious with conviction, correction, and godly counsel or if we spend the whole entire conversation laughing. That is a godly connection.

We sharpen one another and challenge each other to be the best versions of ourselves possible. And most importantly we are moving in the same direction both in purpose and in our spiritual lives. To be completely honest I believe that our friendship was ordained by God because we can't for the life of us even remember when or how we became friends. It just sort of happened. Don't be fooled though, ours is an intentional connection, our friendship is purposeful. That is what a godly connection is more than anything, it's intentional.

If you're in pursuit of purpose, there should be no relationship in your life that's unaccounted for, no relationship in your life without a direction. You don't have time for that. God is an intentional God. He's not just working things out as He goes along. You may be, but He's definitely not. *I make known the end from the beginning, from ancient times, what is still to come. I say, 'My purpose will stand, and I will do all that I please.'* (Isaiah 46:10) God is aware and concerned with everything going on in our lives especially who we connect ourselves to. He has a purpose and a plan even for your relationships.

I pray that God would remove any ungodly connections in your life that would hinder you from realizing your purpose and potential. I encourage you to take inventory of the things and people you have entering and exiting your life. Be intentional about who you spend your time with, it's important, and it makes a difference. If you need godly counsel seek God about finding a mentor, an older woman in the faith, someone who will cover you in prayer and keep it real all at the same time. Find someone you admire and take notes on their success. Don't try to be them, but do try to learn all that you can from their mistakes and triumphs.

Be friends with people you look up to no matter how old they are and keep a unique and diverse group of friends around you because that's how you gain new and unique perspectives. While you're being mentored turn around and mentor someone else, share with them all of the things you wish someone else had told you. In doing this, you can help them to avoid the mistakes you've made and hopefully give them room to make some new errors of their own. And finally, in making Godly connections ask God for discernment to know who to keep close to you and who to keep at a distance because I've seen many a life wasted or ruined based on bad connections to people who looked like friends but operated like enemies.

God,

guide us in our relationships. Give us the wisdom to walk away from any and everything that does not look or sound like you.

We recognize that our time is precious and that you require that we steward it well so help us to be obedient to the leading of your Holy Spirit in our friendships and other relationships. Teach us to appreciate and love the people you place in our care. As we learn and grow in you and in our purpose, give us the heart to reach back and help someone else.

Teach us to be intentional about how we spend our time and who we spend our time with. Thank you for the godly connections you're sending our way, for the positive influences, and Holy Spirit filled mentors you are molding even right now to enter our lives. Thank you for being an intentional God. We honor you and we thank you.

We ask these things in Jesus's Name.

Amen.

Reflections:

Destiny of a Young Woman

Duchanna Brown

Chapter 12: Be A Good Steward

"His master replied, 'Well done, good and faithful servant! You have been faithful with a few things; I will put you in charge of many things. Come and share your master's happiness!'

~Matthew 23:25~

Well, we're at the end. I want to thank you for going on this journey with me and congratulate you on being one step closer to your purpose. As we come to an end I want to leave you with some questions you should ask yourself about your purpose. Can you be trusted with your purpose? Can God trust you with all that He has placed inside of you? Can He expect a return on His investment or should He give what He has for you to someone else who sees its value and will take care of it?

This last chapter has been named and renamed more than once. It's been rethought and reimagined a few times, so finally I told God that if He didn't give it to me, it wouldn't get done. And then, when I was just about to close my eyes and go to bed it hit me. It was something He had brought to my attention in my own life, the importance of being a good steward of what He's given me so I could be entrusted with more. This is a biblical principle that is often applied to finances, but it can be applied to every area of our lives. I'll focus on purpose.

If you're faithful over the "little" things God's given you He'll make you ruler over more. I put the word little in quotes because if we're honest our little is much to someone else. However, if we can't appreciate the little God has given to us He can't give us more, we'll mismanage and abuse it because we don't recognize it's worth to us. We'll take for granted the "next" thing because we never took the time to appreciate the "now" thing. Take your relationship status. If you don't appreciate your singleness, you can't possibly enjoy the gift that is marriage because you never paused long enough to realize that being single and having the freedom to pursue your dreams is just as beautiful as a covenant relationship. Both experiences reflect God's goodness but if you're too busy being upset about your lot in life you'll miss the beauty of it all together because you're chasing the idea of marriage rather than its reality.

We often take for granted what an honor it is to be entrusted with things from God. To be trusted by God with purpose is an honor just like getting to trust God with your purpose is. The fact that He is at all mindful of us should keep us in a continual state of humility because we are specks of dust in comparison to His awesome awe and wonder. Don't take for granted the family, friends, gifts, and talents that He's given you because they could be in someone else's possession altogether, but it was His good pleasure to entrust them into your care.

In Matthew 23:25, Jesus tells the parable of the Talents. He says that the coming of the Kingdom of God would be like a man going on a journey who *entrusted*, there's that word again, his wealth to his servants. To each, he gave a certain number of talents *according to his ability*. In the Master's absence, two of the servants double their earnings they put what the Master gave them to work and had something to show for it. One of the three, however, spent more time concerned about what he lacked than making the most of what he had. He thought to get more he had to have more. All he had to realize was that what he had was more than enough. That even if all he had to show for his time was another talent to add to the one he had, he still would have more than what he started with. He took the Master's gift for granted.

How do you suppose you'll be grateful for more when you're so miserable with little? How can you multiply more when you can barely manage your little? How could you possibly expect God to elevate you in your purpose on purpose when you're disobedient and barely follow Him down the hallway much less into your destiny? God wants to give us more, but we must be in the posture and position to receive it.

So, what does that position look like? I'm glad you asked. Stewarding in expectation for what's next is saying "NO" to things you would normally say "Yes" to. It looks like walking away from some relationships because if you stay in them, you'll grow complacent and comfortable. It looks like walking away from things that might look nice but don't sound like God's will for your life. Simply put, it looks, sounds, and smells like a sacrifice. You may have you wear the same pair of shoes every day until God provides enough money to buy another pair. It may mean living modestly until you can afford the things you desire. Purpose is going to cost you something, but you stand to gain more than you'll ever lose.

Being a good steward is vital because it builds character in you. It teaches you to possess things but not to allow things to possess you. If you were a good steward over "nothing," you won't worship the things when you get them because you realize that you had a purpose before you had things. You won't worship the car, when you get it, you'll give glory to the God who provided the car because you vividly remember when you had to walk. Being a good steward makes you a good servant as well because you recognize that everything you're a steward over belongs to the Master anyway. Your gifts, your talents, your greatness all comes from the Father. They're on loan, and before long God is going to want a return on His investment in you with interest. Especially when He's made you aware of what He's placed inside of you.

God expects you to be fruitful and multiply. Your fruit should then bear trees which then, in turn, continue to bear fruit. This is the will of God for our lives, but it starts with taking care of what He's already given us. We must water the seeds that have already been planted and treat even the smallest of beginnings as if it were our only shot, our big break. God has a plan and a purpose for your life but it all starts with developing the blueprint He's already given you.

Duchanna Brown

Lord,

we just want to thank you for being our portion. Thank you for the lot that you've given us. Thank you that it was your good pleasure to bless us in the ways that you already have.

God, forgive us if we have taken what you've given us for granted. Forgive us if we've treated the blessings you've bestowed upon us as a curse. Help us not to mismanage what you've blessed us with but Lord help us to value every day we get with all that we have. Help us to see our "little" for the much that it really is. Teach us to use it wisely and to be fruitful and multiply it with interest.

God, thank you for entrusting us with all that you have given us. Help us to be as trustworthy and faithful over it as you are with us. Thank you for the purpose and the plan that you have for our lives. Thank you that as we've reached the end of this book we've only begun to see all that you have in store for our lives. Stir up the gifts you've placed within us.

Thank you for allowing our paths, my own and this reader's, to cross. Allow the words they've read to cause a ripple effect not only in their lives but in the lives of everyone connected to them until whole neighborhoods, communities, counties, districts and states are changed.

Destiny of a Young Woman

We believe you. We trust you and we thank you for who you are. Thank you that we are young women with destiny engraved in our DNA. Let us not leave this Earth until it is fully realized. We love you and we honor you for the more you have in store for our lives.

In Jesus's Name, I pray.

Amen.

Reflections:

Destiny of a Young Woman

Duchanna Brown

Epilogue

Well, Sis, you made it to the end. I'm so proud of you. It was uncomfortable and convicting at times, but we both did it. This of course isn't the end for us. Far from it. This is the beginning of the most magnificent adventure of your life. I can't end this book without offering you a formal invitation, however. If you read through this who book and don't know Jesus as your personal Lord and Savior then you've already forfeited your purpose because He makes all this possible. It's only worth it with Him.

So, say this quick prayer with me:

Lord Jesus, I repent of my sins. Come into my life and make me whole. I accept you as my Lord and Savior.

If you said that prayer with sincerity you have been saved.

Find a good Bible-based church and get involved. Pray and read your Bible and seek the face of God and I promise you, your life will never be the same.

I love you.

God, Bless You.

Now, live on purpose.

About the Author

Duchanna Brown is a vibrant, young author with a passion for empowering young women to be all that God has created them to be. She believes that people matter. She uses this passion to inspire everyone around her to believe first in God and then in themselves so they will can help others.

A Howard University alum she desires to see young people, especially young women, walk in their God given purpose. In August 2017, she pursued her own purpose by returning to school to earn her Master of Divinity at Wesley Theological Seminary in Washington, DC.

This is her first book.

Contact her at:

info.duchannasbook@gmail.com

www.ingramcontent.com/pod-product-compliance
Lightning Source LLC
Chambersburg PA
CBHW030900170426
43193CB00009BA/688